D0382523

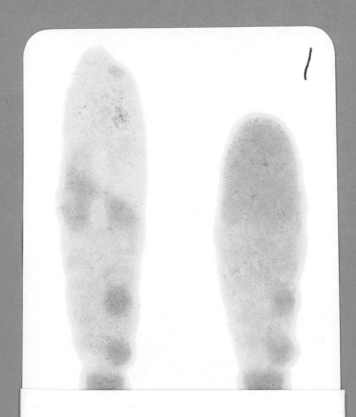

1

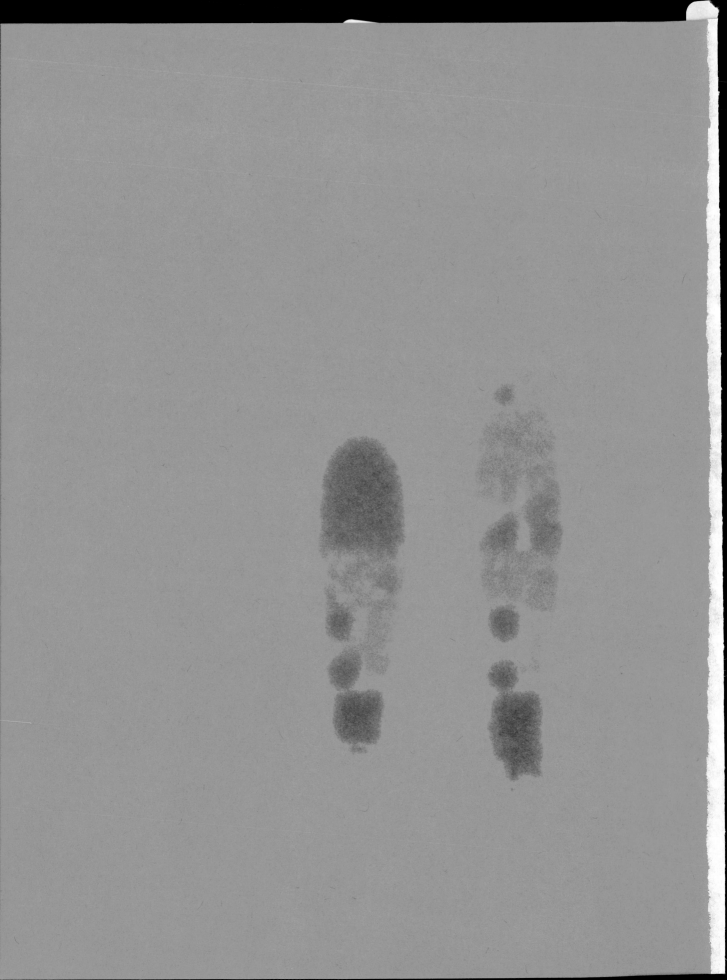

DISCOVERING THE MYSTERIOUS EGRET

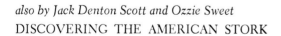

also by Jack Denton Scott and Ozzie Sweet
DISCOVERING THE AMERICAN STORK

DISCOVERING

Words by Jack Denton Scott

Photographs by Ozzie Sweet
with line drawings by Pamela Sweet Distler

THE MYSTERIOUS EGRET

HARCOURT BRACE JOVANOVICH

NEW YORK AND LONDON

Library of Congress Cataloging in Publication Data

Scott, Jack Denton
    Discovering the mysterious egret.

    SUMMARY: Describes what limited information is
known about the habits of the enigmatic cattle egret
which has migrated to every continent from its native
Africa.
    1. Cattle egret—Juvenile literature.   [1. Cattle
egret. 2. Herons] I. Sweet, Ozzie.   II. Distler,
Pamela.   III. Title.
QL696.C52S28   598.3′4   77–88967
ISBN 0–15–223593–0

Picture credits, pages viii-1-2, 7 and 27, Marcia C. Gauger

First edition

B C D E F G H I J K

Peering down from high ground in East Africa, the immense strange land where many believe that man was born, at the broad floor of the Rift Valley, one's eyes are magnetically drawn upward to the distant peaks of Mount Kenya, towering like cloud pillars through purple haze to 17,000 feet. As the eyes turn slowly downward again they catch sight of a mass movement, a shifting, as if parts of the floor of the valley are sliding away. It is made by the cattle of the Masai, grazing in large herds. The tall and haughty people of this unique African tribe believe that their god gave them exclusive rights to all the cattle in the world, and their primary diet consists of the milk and the blood of these cattle that they so carefully guard and protect from wild predators.

Occasionally there appear to be butterfly bursts above the cattle, white fans in motion hovering over them. If one looks carefully through binoculars, these unfurling fans are seen to be birds of the purest white, falling now to earth like a snowstorm among the slow-moving herds.

The birds, necks thrust forward in a weaving, gooselike motion, follow the cattle closely as they move, staying mere inches from their feet. Occasionally, an animal stops chomping the grass and swings its head around at a nearby bird. But the bird doesn't move a feather or change its stance at the motion.

A Masai herdsman in a cloak, his glistening black hair plaited into pigtails, carries a long spear and a shield made of animal hide dyed orange and black, and stands guard over the herd. He allows the cattle to move fifty yards forward before he slowly walks abreast of them. The Masai is alert, eyes roving everywhere. A lion frequently comes charging to pick off straggling cattle, so the herdsman lingers behind with a purpose. He has already proved his mettle and his manhood according to tribal custom, which demands that, armed only with spear and shield, he slay a cattle-killing lion.

The great Rift Valley

Now, almost idly, as if playing an old game, the young warrior shakes his spear at a white bird walking sedately beside a cow. The bird merely flutters up from the ground onto the back of the animal and stays there.

Closer to the jungles, miles away from the Kenya plains and the Masai, a hippopotamus has just waded from a river and its daily mud bath. The mud is streaked on its sun-faded gray hide like paint. As it moves ponderously along the land by the river edge, it is followed by the same kind of white bird that followed the Masai cattle.

Not far from this turgid African river, another huge creature stands regarding a clump of heavy growth from which it has just emerged. It is a rhinoceros, an ugly, fearsome animal with a horn of bone jutting from its nose, which suddenly clumps away from the bushy area, its great feet raising miniature dirt clouds as it moves. Unafraid of this grotesque ton of flesh that could crush it into a puff of feathers, yet another of the white birds serenely walks beside the gigantic feet.

. . . the hippopotamus (above) . . . the rhinoceros (right) . . .

Why has nature encouraged such strange relationships? Is this an instance of symbiosis in which bird and animal collaborate to their mutual advantage, or is their association one in which only the bird benefits (commensalism)?

One fact is certain: this bird, *Bubulus ibis*, a unique member of the heron family, has been following large, hoofed animals around the grasslands of Africa for many thousands of years. Fossil remains date it as far back as the Pleistocene epoch, so it was living near plain and jungle long before modern man appeared on earth.

No one seems to know when this beautiful white heron—sometimes called buff-backed heron, cattle heron, or tick heron—first got the name "cattle egret." However, it does seem to prefer cattle, both domesticated and wild, such as the Cape and water buffaloes, although it is often seen riding the backs of Africa's largest mammals, the elephants.

. . . the Cape buffalo

While perched on the backs of these various beasts, cattle egrets have been observed picking off ticks and other bothersome insects. Thus there may be mutual benefits, though birdmen believe the relationship is mainly a one-sided affair, the bird being the major benefactor. These clever birds, unlike all other herons, do not have to work very hard for what they seek—*food*.

As the large animals graze and walk through grasslands, they flush out great numbers of insects, especially grasshoppers. Following the animals closely, the cattle egrets lazily dine on these insects, their main diet. Researchers have concluded, from counting footsteps and insects taken, that the cattle egret expends amazingly little energy in catching the food it eats. In the few instances when the bird does feed alone, without benefit of its partner's large, insect-raising feet, it must scurry about for long periods before it can find enough food to satisfy its appetite.

Some naturalists formerly believed that the cattle egret was of service to its hosts by acting as a sentry—while the ani-

mals were grazing, the birds on their backs would spot danger from afar, and utter cries of alarm. Called "protocooperation," these relationships are well known. A few other birds, such as the oxpecker (which maintains a similar relationship with the rhinoceros, buffalo, giraffe, and antelope) and the African oxpecker (which feeds off pest insects on animals' backs, ridding them of the parasites) do warn, with shrill alarm cries, of approaching danger, especially from hunters. Recent studies, however, seem to show that the cattle egret does not perform this service—at least not by any design of nature's.

Actually, very little is known about the cattle egret. Only within the last few years has a detailed study been made about the bird, and even that summarized it as "mysterious."

Certainly it is known that Africa is its homeland, its major breeding ground. There it is seen everywhere from veld country to jungle and even in public parks near cities. It is also known that the cattle egret is a nomad and that some of the birds began leaving Africa centuries ago.

The cattle egret . . .

. . . in Africa . . .

Why did they leave Africa at all? No one can say definitely, although some have suggested that there may have been a cattle egret population explosion that forced the birds to find new feeding grounds. But the great continent of Africa, with its vast grasslands and huge herds of wild animals, is surely large enough to support even an immense quantity of the birds. So some biologists have explained their appearance in Spain, in southeast Asia and Australia, and as far north as Japan as "gypsying," an instinct to travel, to move, to colonize in new areas. Simple wanderlust.

No one was prepared, however, for what happened one sunny day in 1930, when herdsmen in British Guiana looked up and saw a flock of strange birds come spinning out of the sky. Shining like alabaster, they fluttered down among the herds of grazing Brahman cattle. As if by prearranged signal, each bird in the flock selected its own cow to walk beside.

Cattle egrets had arrived in South America!

Less than twenty years later, the birds had spread throughout Surinam, Venezuela, and Colombia, until in some areas no bird of comparable size could match them in numbers. And no bird of any species, regardless of size, was as conspicuous in the Cauca Valley of Colombia, where each dawn thousands of egrets left their colonies to feed in the pastures with the cattle. They had conquered their new world quickly, and apparently without difficulty.

. . . and South America

The well-known ornithologist Roger Tory Peterson, an early student of this fascinating bird, speculated in 1954 in the *National Geographic* about their astonishing arrival in South America:

"How did they come? Could they be descendants of birds that had escaped from some zoo, perhaps the one at Georgetown, British Guiana? We ornithologists have no evidence to prove such a hypothesis. Did someone deliberately introduce them from abroad? Not likely, for surely there would be some record of such a project.

"Did [they] reach South America as stowaways, perhaps on a cattle boat? Even this is unlikely, for a number of avian hitchhikers would have had to make the journey to provide a nucleus for successful breeding.

"The most plausible theory, it seems, is that the birds were wind-borne. The Atlantic is 1,770 miles wide between the bulge of Africa and northern South America, and the birds are good flyers. Assisted by strong winds from the east, they could conceivably have covered the distance before they were completely exhausted."

Peterson concludes that if the cattle egrets indeed made this remarkable flight to the New World, that it would be the *only* bird from the Old World in history to establish residence in the two Americas without human aid. "All the other foreign birds which have taken up residence here within historical times were introduced by man."

As the cattle egret's range expanded over much of northern South America and southward into Brazil, puzzled scientists began to study it earnestly. Birds and animals that have greatly increased their natural ranges without the help of man are undeniably examples of biological success. By close scrutiny of these accomplishments, by study of the creatures in their new locations, man may find answers to some of the complicated questions about the processes of evolution.

Introducing itself to . . .

. . . a Brahman bull . . .

But for many years natural scientists were able to draw few conclusions about this remarkable feathered immigrant. Bird books that contain much detail on other members of the heron family have sparse information on the cattle egret. Until recently, out of its fifty behavioral patterns, forty were unknown.

The bird confused the experts. It kept popping up where least expected. And no one could successfully explain how it got there. Was this a new species, an explorer bird periodically and methodically flying out of Africa in search of new lands? If so, why? This was not migration; what was it? Immigration, yes. But for what purpose? No one knew. Bird experts knew of no other bird that behaved in this fashion, no other bird that could fly so far, adapt so fast, and achieve breeding and colonizing success so quickly and apparently so easily.

The next dramatic move of this enigmatic vagabond stunned even the most experienced and imaginative of ornithologists.

At five-thirty on the morning of April 23, 1952, three experienced birdwatchers—William H. Drury, Jr., Allen Morgan, and Richard Stackpole—drove to Sudbury Valley in Massachusetts to count the numbers and varieties of ducks and spring migrants. They were excited when, near Heard Pond, on the Erwin farm, they discovered a glossy ibis, a dark-feathered heronlike bird with a long down-swooping bill. And with good reason—this was the first time a glossy ibis had been seen in Sudbury Valley for over a hundred years.

After they had jotted down field notes, time of discovery, and points of identification, they were about to leave the pond when Morgan saw a bird drop in among a herd of cows a few hundred yards away. Without putting binoculars to his eyes, he called out, "Snowy egret! It shouldn't be here. Too early. We've made a double today!"

Beside him, Drury raised binoculars and focused in on the bird.

"No! It's . . . it's a *cattle* egret!" he whispered in amazement. He had seen the birds several years ago in the Guianas.

Morgan, who had a federal collecting permit, rushed to the farmhouse and telephoned Ludlow Griscom, the leading field ornithologist in New England, urging him to come immediately to help identify the bird before they "collected" it.

"This is a first in North America!" Griscom said excitedly. "Don't wait for me! Collect the bird immediately for the scientific record!"

Ornithological rules dictate that the first record of arrival of a new species in an unusual geographical area must be proved by killing and presenting a specimen. Though all three of these field ornithologists had misgivings about this protocol, this was the way it had to be done, to provide proof positive

. . . an Angus cow . . .

that this amazing bird had appeared in the United States. From where? Spain? South America? Africa, after several stops? How and why weren't presently important. The fact was that it was here!

The birdmen themselves also feared that no one would believe their report. It did not seem possible that this fragile bundle of feathers could have crossed the stormy northern route of the Atlantic Ocean to reach Sudbury Valley. What would other ornithologists say?

There was no time to worry about that. But securing that first specimen in the United States nearly turned into a comedy of errors.

Proving that it was indeed a cattle egret, the white bird stayed close to the head of the grazing heifer it had selected to follow. Shooing the cow away from the bird and using a borrowed shotgun, Drury—they think it was Drury, but they were so excited that no one is certain—managed to get off two shots. He missed with both barrels.

Flying as swiftly as a dove, the cattle egret took off over the apple orchard heading for the next farm, several miles away. Stackpole quieted the fears of the others by telling them that this farm had a large herd of Aberdeen Angus cattle, which would surely attract the cattle egret. He reasoned that the bird must have just completed a long flight, that it was hungry, hadn't had time to satisfy its appetite, and would be tempted to land and feed among the cattle.

It was a plausible theory, but it didn't work. They found no herd of cattle and no cattle egret.

Frustrated, fearful that they would lose the bird and the honor that would go with securing the first of this exotic species, they drove to the nearby home of a friend who had a Piper Cub. Shortly after 6:00 A.M. they rousted the pilot out of bed and talked him into helping them.

One of the birdwatchers went with the pilot; the other two drove. Flying low, the two in the plane soon spotted the white bird in a farmyard. Zooming down over the car, they relayed the location. But by the time the car got there, the cattle egret was gone. This went on for another hour, until finally the bird was hedged in, the plane buzzing overhead to try to keep it out of the air, one of the field ornithologists boxing it in with the car on one side, the third lumbering toward it in a borrowed tractor.

Finally, with the combined forces of four men, an airplane, an automobile, and a tractor, the cattle egret's presence in Massachusetts became a fact. Now the bird could be officially added to the North American list in the Museum of Comparative Zoology at Harvard University.

But, as anticipated, there was skepticism. Ornithologists claimed that it just wasn't possible for the bird to fly from Africa, Spain, or even South America. The obvious explanation was that it had escaped from a nearby zoo. A careful check, however, proved that no cattle egret had ever inhabited a New England zoo.

. . . and calf

All doubts were wiped away when, in early May, another cattle egret was discovered on the McPherson farm in Cape May, New Jersey. A few days later, still another appeared on that farm. These, of course, were not "collected"; the birds were protected. Birdwatchers poured in from all over the eastern United States to see the two African visitors that had discovered America.

Then, on June 1, Louis A. Stimson, a veteran ornithologist, ambling along the shores of Lake Okeechobee, Florida, startled ten white birds gathered in two groups of four and six. He immediately identified them as members of the heron family, then as egrets, perhaps snowy egrets. But snowies are skittery, nervous; these birds let him walk very close to them before they lazily took off—so close that birdwatcher Stimson was able to identify them correctly as cattle egrets.

The newcomer seems more at ease than the New Jersey cow.

Stimson knew that he was seeing the glamorous new immigrants when he realized that the birds were not, as they had at first appeared, pure white like several of our native egrets. Only cattle egrets have an almost orange-buff coloring on backs, breasts, and crowns during the mating season. In the brilliant Florida sunshine these birds looked as if they were touched with gold.

They were here then, the Africans! And in breeding plumage! That led to one conclusion: they were going to establish in this region. Perhaps they had already established, and no one had noticed.

Early in 1953 a cattle egret nest was discovered at the south end of Lake Okeechobee, not far from Clewiston. In less than two years the invasion was in full force; a thousand pairs were nesting there, and, to the delight of birdwatchers, the birds were turning up in pastures and near waterways all over Florida.

Oddly, though, the cattle egrets did not come like strangers into this new land. Seemingly without hesitation, they had flown to the mangrove and cypress groves in isolated, swampy places like Corkscrew Swamp Sanctuary and Pelican Island, where they settled in as if they had lived there forever. These are protected areas, and, as with all acts of these enigmatic birds, there seemed to have been a master plan, a pattern to this immigration, this mass movement. They had roosted and built rookeries where they were *safe*.

They also had the perfect camouflage: white on white. Only the experts would be able to tell that a new breed of birds was here, for they were so much like some of the wading birds that had lived in the region for years that their arrival could have gone unnoticed.

Andrew J. Meyerrieck, professor of ornithology at the University of South Florida, believes that, in fact, cattle egrets may have been in Florida, unrecognized, since the 1930s. It was the publicity given the discovery of the birds in Massachusetts and New Jersey that alerted birdmen in Florida to search carefully among the white wading birds for the Africans.

To strengthen Professor Meyerrieck's theory, an experienced birder, Willard E. Dilley, of Homestead, Florida, claimed to have seen a pair of cattle egrets east of Clewiston in the early 1940s. He said that he hadn't reported his discovery because he had thought they must have escaped from captivity nearby.

Wildlife photographer Richard Borden discovered that he had photographed cattle egrets in Florida on March 12, 1952. He had thought they were snowy egrets and had not been sure of their true identity until it was pointed out to him by Roger Tory Peterson.

Borden's announcement set birdmen to narrowing the points of identification. Cattle egrets are not wading birds, even though they are closely related to that large and diverse group that needs to live near the water where its feeding activities

Kin and kinship in the Corkscrew Swamp Sanctuary

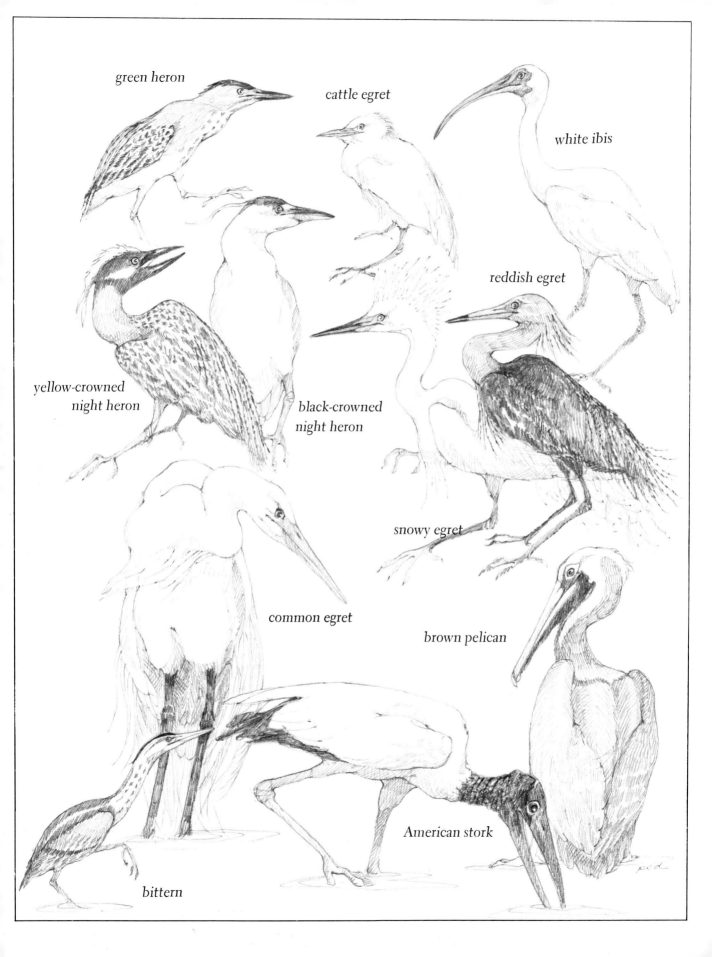

green heron

cattle egret

white ibis

reddish egret

yellow-crowned
night heron

black-crowned
night heron

snowy egret

common egret

brown pelican

bittern

American stork

center. Nor could the cattle egrets be confused with such species as the long-billed wood stork, the brown pelican, the small dark bittern, the yellow-crowned or the black-crowned night heron, the green heron, nor, even though they are the same color, with the white ibis, since all these birds have distinctive long curved bills and black-tipped wings.

The cattle egret's "cousins," which confused the sight picture, are not at all mysterious and have been long-time residents of the land near the waterways. Five of them are white or have white phases and from a distance, or at certain times of the year, might be mistaken for the newcomer.

Size should have eliminated some cases of mistaken identity. The cattle egret is about twenty inches in length. The great white heron is fifty inches long and has a seven-foot wing spread and a tuft on the back of its head, though, like the cattle egret, it has a yellow bill and yellow legs and feet. To add to the confusion, this large bird is also thought by some bird experts to be a white phase of the great blue heron.

The common egret (also known as the American egret and a large, majestic bird) has a habitat covering the whole of Florida. It is forty inches in length and has a yellow bill, but its legs are black.

The reddish egret, twenty-nine inches long, is nearer the size of the cattle egret but has a shaggy head, a flesh-colored bill, and dark, bronze-brown feathers. In its immature phase, however, it has white plumage.

The snowy egret may have produced the most confusion. Even though it is twenty-two inches long, with black bill and legs and tufts of feathers on its head, from any distance it is difficult to distinguish from the cattle egret. And the twenty-two-inch little blue heron with bluish bill and greenish legs, in its pure white immature phase, might also be mistaken for the newcomer, especially when roosting or nesting.

The cattle egret, however, despite the complication of other white egrets, is a distinctive character. Only about twenty inches long, its bill yellow, its legs and feet yellow, pinkish, greenish, or blackish, it is stockier than any other heron. It is short-necked, and that neck is almost never held in the graceful curve of all others of the family, but is extended straight, diagonally upward or forward (to nearly horizontal), or sometimes drawn in to the shoulders. Also the cattle egret's feathers give its throat a sort of puffed appearance. And the unmistakable mark of identification that vividly brands it during the breeding season are the rusty-buff feathers on the back of the head, the breast, and the back.

Its flight is also different from the other herons, being more abrupt and rapid, with the wings making a smaller beating arc, while the others have a more stately, leisurely flight.

Of the sixty-four species of herons, egrets, and bitterns worldwide, only thirteen are found in North America. Herons and egrets are classified as long-legged, long-necked wading birds with lean body lines and very graceful movements. Some people confuse herons and egrets with cranes. But in flight they are easy to distinguish. Cranes fly with necks extended. Herons and egrets carry their necks in a graceful S curve—except the cattle egret, the bird that is the exception to most of the rules of its race.

Egrets may be further divided from herons by calling them "plume-bearing herons." Their fancy curled feathers, called aigrettes, once nearly doomed the common and the snowy egrets. The sparkling white feathers, which used to decorate women's hats, are part of a nuptial train of fifty-four feathers trailing down the common egret's back. In the early 1900s, plume hunters received thirty-two dollars an ounce for those aigrettes, at that time almost double the price of gold. Federal law finally protected all herons and egrets from what one ornithologist called "man's greed and woman's vanity."

The cattle egret, growing no aigrettes, never had that problem; in fact, it seems, in all aspects, a problem-free bird. Even its mating, breeding, and raising young seem acts programmed for survival.

The cattle egrets came to the cypresses of Corkscrew Swamp Sanctuary, and to the stunted mangroves of Pelican Island, in stages. There was no forthright invasion of large flocks fluttering in. The birds came singly, in twos and threes, in flocks of a dozen. Still, no one knew from where they came. Africa, Spain, South America? Had they landed in many places in New England and along the east coast and just hadn't been observed, or been mistaken for other white egrets? Then, being accustomed to a warm climate, had they finally selected Florida as the perfect place to reproduce their species?

"The birds came singly, in two and threes . . ."

Those who know the cattle egret and are aware of its success in Florida wonder about its timing. It seemed to have waited until conditions were just right before it immigrated. For many years Florida had no large, hoofed animals. Deer, yes, but these were forest dwellers, not the plains and grassland species that the bird preferred. Finally, as Florida was developed, settlers brought in cattle and horses. In time, the state became one of the important livestock areas in the country, with many ranches and much pasture land: cattle egret country.

Through the filmy half-light of dawn, the birds fly to the pastures and to the cattle, returning at dusk, as they do wherever they live. They leave the groves of trees deep in swampland quietly; they have no argument with the long-establishd residents; they cause no disturbance; they do not confiscate too much territory.

In the Florida rookeries of the waterbirds, a flock of wood storks spirals and circles overhead, forming a flapping halo of long necks and outstretched legs; white and glossy ibis wing beneath them, clacking long, slender bills at the brown pelicans as they flap from the trees, then soar on air currents like sailplanes. Common egrets, snowy egrets, Louisiana herons, as well as anhingas with their long, snaky necks, roost and build nests within feet of the cattle egrets. In April sunshine shiny-white cattle egrets clustered in one tree gleam like lighted candles in a candelabrum.

There is no competition for territory. Cattle egret colonies are compact and do not sprawl into the areas of the other birds. One hundred cattle egret nests in a single tree are not unusual, and observers have counted as many as three hundred. Thus, unlike many birds that roost and nest without regard for their neighbors or without properly utilizing space, cattle egrets are conservative colonizers.

White cattle egrets clustered in a tree

One more reason for cattle egret superiority is their long breeding season, which can run, in Florida, from April through July. With numbers of birds breeding periodically throughout these months, survival of at least some offspring is insured, despite the heavy wind and rainstorms that often destroy the eggs and young of species of egrets and wading birds that have a limited breeding season. If torrential spring rains flood the nests of pairs of cattle egrets that have bred in April, destroying eggs and nestlings, other pairs breeding the next month will successfully add the necessary numerical strength for the survival of the species.

"In the Florida
rookeries
of the waterbirds..."

The mating of these birds is also a singular session. As described earlier, cattle egrets ready for it have buff feathers on head, chest, and back. In Florida the color appears in April when the birds begin looking for mates. Before the formation of pairs, which appear to mate for life, the male selects a "display area" that he permits no other bird to enter.

The ways that the unmated male shows his sexual aggression have been carefully detailed by Dr. Douglas A. Lancaster, director of the Laboratory of Ornithology at Cornell University, who studied at length a cattle egret colony in Colombia, South America. He observed that the cattle egret male has his own peculiar stances and threatening displays during this pre-mating period.

The male in the mating mood "feather postures" with wings hanging slightly down and open, the mouth often gaping, the feathers on the neck and head erect.

In the "forward-threat" the bird stretches his neck and head forward and upward at a forty-five-degree angle, his neck forming a shallow U shape. He points his bill up; feathers on his crown flare. If any other bird moves close, the feathers on the displaying male's neck become fully erect, and he slashes with his beak, uttering a harsh *raa raa* call. Sometimes that call softens to a *kerr kerr* just before both the defender and the contester leap into the air like fighting cocks—which they are.

In his selected site, the displaying male makes a number of motions, signaling not only that he is defending his area but also that he is ready to mate. The signals include the "stretch," the "forward-snap," the "wing-touch," the "flapflight," and the "twig-shake."

In the "stretch," the male extends his neck vertically, holding the bill at about a seventy-five-degree angle off the horizontal, the body at fifty degrees. Partially withdrawing head and neck into his shoulders, he then flexes his legs and lowers his breast so that it almost touches the perch. As he makes this bow,

stretch

forward-snap

wing-touch

twig-shake

flap-flight

the plumes on his back spring erect and spread laterally. As he comes upright again, he makes several soft *rooo rooo* crooning notes.

This seduction behavior and language do not seem to be, as displays so often are in the bird world, aimed at any particular female. The male on his chosen perch goes through the motions of attracting a mate almost as if he were entertaining the entire colony. In fact, although his instincts force him to make this performance, he seems to have no interest whatsoever in any female. His sole purpose appears to be aggression toward all.

The "forward-snap" appears to be just a desultory action, unlike the "forward-threat," in which the bird makes violent slashing motions. The male's feathers are also erect, but this display is often a single half-hearted stab, with the neck extended, then withdrawn.

The "wing-touch" is a preening motion, usually a single rapid sweep, drawing the open bill along the leading edge of one wing. But sometimes the egret will repeat this motion with the other wing.

"Flap-flight" is an aerial display, performed when the egret gets very close to choosing a mate, and may continue for several days. Suddenly the male will leap off his perch in his selected site, fly to a tree fifty feet away, then circle and come back to the original perch. Wing beats are slow, stately, exaggerated, loudly "thumping" against the bird's body, with legs dangling diagonally behind and below, the neck extended, held above the horizontal body, the feathers of the neck and the crown fully erect.

The "twig-shake" may be the most frequent action. The male stretches his neck as far as he can toward a twig or even a leaf above or below him, seizes it with his bill, then shakes it with a series of fast head movements lasting about two seconds. Feathers on neck and crest are erect during this display. Dr.

Lancaster thought that the twig-shake was perhaps part of the nest-building behavior, out of context, since the movements are like those shown by both male and female while working on a nest.

What does all this twig-shaking, bill-slashing, cock-fighting, feather-stiffening, and stately flap-flight accomplish? It brings the females, sometimes as many as a dozen, to within ten feet. Curiously, though, for four or five hours, or even for several days, the displaying male will drive off any other cattle egret, male or female, that comes close to him.

The formation of the pair is finally accomplished by an aggressive female. She circles, comes upon the male from behind, her crest feathers erect, and lands squarely on his back, balancing there long enough to peck the male's head until his own aggressive manner vanishes.

If, however, the female does not remain on the male's back long enough to subdue him, or if he turns in time to prevent her from landing on his back, a violent fight ensues, on the perch, even on the ground, and the female is driven off. If successful, after her initial pecking violence, the female will stand on the male's back for several minutes, rubbing her bill against the side of his neck and face, gently taking feathers from his crest in her bill, and often lightly grasping his head or his neck.

Once the male is quiet and submits to her caresses, she dismounts and turns her attention to driving away any other females that may come in and try to take advantage of the work she has done.

Observers have been amused to see females sizing up males, watching their displays with obvious, head-cocking interest, then finally selecting a male that had chosen a site where a nest was already built. In most cases, in fact, males that displayed on branches where there was already an abandoned nest outdrew those who carried on their appealing antics on a perch where there was no nest.

The courtship behavior may be unusual and dramatic, but what happens to the color of the mating birds as their hormones are set into motion during the breeding season is nothing short of fantastic. William J. Weber, a veterinarian who has studied a colony of cattle egrets on Lake Griffin in central Florida for several years, has described the remarkable change in the cattle egret's appearance that almost overnight makes it seem to be a completely different bird.

When the birds first show interest in mating, their color, except for the buff feathers, is normal: yellow beaks, yellow skin around the eyes, yellow spaces between the eye and the beak, yellow eye irises. But within days the bill begins to turn red, and twenty-four hours after the first red tinge appears, it becomes a vivid scarlet with a shiny golden tip. All exposed skin flushes scarlet and red-purple, the irises become brilliant red with a ring of yellow, and the yellow-green or blackish legs change to a vivid Chinese red. The white heron becomes a tropical beauty.

These fast and startling changes occur in both male and female, and as there is little difference in size, it is impossible to tell the sexes apart. But mating display actions do mark the male, as does the actual breeding, for the male, as with other birds, is the one treading atop the female.

Breeding does not occur, however, until a nest site has been chosen and usually takes place while the nest is being constructed. If a nest is already intact, the breeding begins immediately.

The nest building is teamwork, which continues throughout the raising of the family. And now that the pair has mated, both fiercely defend the limited territory immediately around the nest, which may be less than a foot or as much as six feet. The male delivers the twigs and the female builds the nest, not very skillfully, but adequately, with the male making many twig-carrying trips. Building time varies from two days to a week. The completed nest ranges from ten to eighteen inches in diameter and three to nine inches in depth.

While construction is underway, the male signals his desire to breed by seizing a heavy twig and vigorously shaking it, continuing until he attracts the female's attention. She responds with loud calls, flying to the nest area, where the male mounts her for about six seconds. This is repeated several times. He then flies to a branch and preens himself, then gets back to the business of building the nest, bringing a variety of twigs, the female selecting the larger ones to make the foundation. A typical nest contains two hundred large sticks and sixty small twigs, a sturdy but, compared to the tightly woven nests of some birds, an unprofessional-looking job.

Now that the nest is ready, so is the female. Every other day she lays a light-blue egg. Sometimes the total is two, sometimes three or four, rarely five. With the laying of the first egg comes another dramatic physical change. Male and female undergo such a fast color fade that within two days all of the brilliant red color has gone from bills, skin, and legs, leaving only an orange tinge on the legs which also vanishes in another two days.

Egg laying begins . . .

As the egg laying begins, one bird is always at the nest to prevent predation and insure that the reproduction will be successful.

When all the eggs are laid, the pair shares incubation duties. The hatching, like the laying, occurs in two-day intervals, with all the eggs hatched within twenty-four days. Each chick weighs two-thirds of an ounce.

The first-hatched chick has the usual struggle to pierce the shell wall of the egg with its egg-tooth, then laboriously cracks away the shell bit by bit, until it is free. But the first-born also has an obvious advantage. As it is the first to eat, it begins growing immediately and maintains a size superiority over the other chicks, becoming twice as large as the second-born, three times the size of the third. If there are four chicks,

. . . and hatching follows . . .

the last born has a slow growth rate and is usually starved and eventually shoved out of the nest by the others.

This staggered egg laying and hatching enable the cattle egrets always to have at least one healthy chick survive. If conditions are normal, two nestlings are raised successfully; if food is very abundant and the weather perfect, three chicks may make it out of the nest to maturity. Almost never do four survive. However, even when weather conditions are bad and food is short, a pair of cattle egrets can always successfully raise their first-born chick. Working on the immutable law of survival that dictates that food availability is the principal factor in who will live and who will die, cattle egrets demonstrate that it is better to raise one healthy offspring rather than three weak ones. Thus, they insure that the survivor is vigorous and healthy, which is proper to perpetuate the species.

. . . one by one

Neighboring baby pelicans, American wood storks, and cattle egrets fill the air with their demands for food.

Both parents feed and brood the nestlings. At first they feed the chicks by regurgitating food into their open bills. Later they touch the offsprings' bills with a food bolus or wad, which the young peck. Food that isn't eaten is reswallowed by the adults. But that rarely happens. Cattle egret chicks are ravenous and aggressive, soon learning not to wait for the bolus to be dropped in the nest but reaching up and grasping the parent's bill and yanking its head down, so that the food is dropped directly into their mouths.

Within days they can swallow wads of food larger than their own heads, and as they grow, they become so aggressive that they actually fight their parents to get the food from them. Unlike many young birds, cattle egrets can recognize their parents among the hundreds that are flying in and out of the nesting colony and often rush to meet them, crying loudly for food. They are fed by their parents for about six weeks. In forty days the fledglings can fly a few feet, in another ten days flap short distances, and at the end of two months fly well enough to accompany their parents to the feeding grounds.

Those feeding grounds are perhaps what has made the cattle egret one of the most successful birds in the world. In the United States it may be the most successful, especially since no other bird has ever filled the niche that the cattle egret now occupies.

That niche, in the pastures wherever there is livestock, is occupied only by these unique birds that have learned to let others do most of their food finding. As in other countries, one to three cattle egrets walk beside each animal—cow, horse, sheep, or goat—sometimes one on each side and always one near its head, and each bird will defend its own territory against other trespassing egrets. These birds are so adaptable that they even follow tractors and mowing machines and have been seen taking advantage of grass fires that drive out insects. They also search newly plowed fields for grubs and larvae.

Ornithologist Meyerrieck says that, where no cattle were present, he has seen groups of the birds leapfrogging over one another as they worked their way across a field. In this manner those in front stirred up insects for the ones in back.

Dr. Meyerrieck even observed cooperation between cattle and egrets. He saw a bull lying and chewing its cud and periodically turning its head toward a nearby cattle egret, flaring its nostrils, and permitting the bird to reach in with its bill and snatch flies.

In that "associative feeding behavior" with cattle, the birds have been observed running frantically to keep up with their hoofed hosts, and when the cattle rested, so did the birds, sometimes for hours at a time.

Other observers, however, also saw cattle egrets wading in shallow water looking for fish as the other herons do. This behavior, plus the fact that experts soon discovered that in Florida cattle egrets appeared to be more numerous than all the native species of herons combined, led to a fear that the strangers were perhaps competing with native herons for food. With their swift growth in population, this could become a crucial factor. Were the cattle egrets also becoming wading birds and eating the same food as the American birds?

To make matters worse, some field ornithologists claimed that they had seen cattle egrets eating the young of ground-nesting birds.

The worried birdmen had also thought that the cattle egrets would overpopulate the rookeries of native birds and push them out of living space. But those fears proved groundless. Cattle egrets kept to their own compact colonies.

Wading in shallow water

Michael J. Fogarty, a biologist with the Florida Game and Fresh Water Fish Commission, was assigned the task of making an involved study of the food habits of the cattle egrets. He carefully identified the food from the stomachs of 841 cattle egrets from four roosts in north-central Florida. The study, made dur-

ing the summer, proved conclusively that the cattle egrets were not infringing upon the food sources of the other herons and wading birds. The biologist's report showed that 80 percent of the cattle egret diet consisted of grasshoppers, crickets, spiders, flies, and beetles. Earthworms and cricket frogs were also eaten, but not fish of any kind, and no young of ground-nesting birds.

Insect hunting

The conclusion was an obvious one. Not only was the cattle egret not competing with the other herons and egrets, but it was occupying a food position that was not being used by any other bird. It was also discovered that many of the insects the birds were eating were of varieties that were in some ways harmful to man—that, in fact, the cattle egret was functioning in the biological control of these insects and thus was beneficial.

William J. Weber, the veterinarian who appears to know more about the cattle egret than most of the ornithologists, believes that not only is feeding technique a main ecological reason for the rapid spread of the species, but also that the cattle egret's breeding routine is important. Nesting stability, the incubating, brooding, and constant feeding of the young by both parents, the dominant survival order of the young, based on available food, and the long breeding season add up to an evolutionary balance that favors certain survival for the cattle egret.

In short, the remarkable cattle egret is a startling biological success that is rapidly spreading all over the northern hemisphere. Today these birds are found everywhere in Florida and throughout most of the eastern states, along the Gulf Coast into Texas, west to California and Washington, and even in New Brunswick and Newfoundland in Canada. They have also been seen in Australia. The bird is now found in every continent of the world.

Do they migrate? Probably, but their routes are not known. It is believed that there is spring and fall movement to and from the United States mainland through the Florida Keys, perhaps from Cuba.

Dr. Meyerrieck, conducting banding experiments on young cattle egrets, found that most hatchlings stayed in the vicinity of the nest during their first summer. But, again, with cattle egrets there is no hard-and-fast rule. Some of the young dispersed immediately in every compass direction and were seen many miles

from their hatching area. After migrating back to Florida, these wanderers may have returned to new colonies the next year to breed. As the result of his banding experiments, Dr. Meyerrieck thinks that the cattle egrets expand their range by fanning out from centers of abundance such as Florida and establishing new colonies in other areas. But no one can explain with scientific certainty how the birds could have established themselves so far from their original African homeland.

Recently a fledgling banded at Lake Okeechobee, Florida, was shot in December of the same year at Quintana Roo, on the Yucatan peninsula of Mexico. A lone scout seeking new lands to conquer? And why leave Florida, the warm land of plenty?

No one knows, as no one knew why the birds left Africa for South America, or South America for North America. This enigmatic gypsy bird, this intriguing white nomad, is still shrouded in mystery and may always be.

A lone scout?

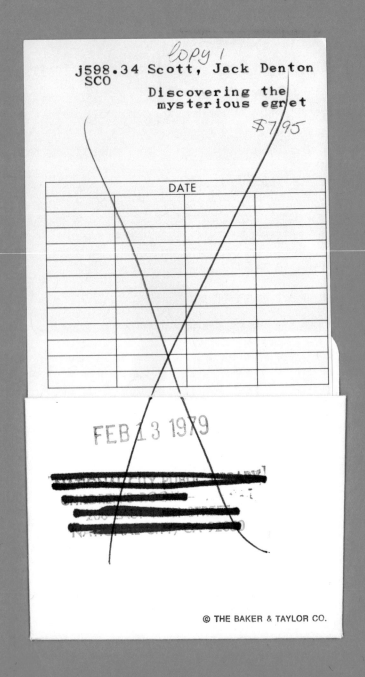

copy 1

j598.34 Scott, Jack Denton
SCO
Discovering the
mysterious egret

$7.95

DATE		

FEB 13 1979